AN OCEAN OF STATIC

J.R. Carpenter is a Canadian-born, UK-based artist, writer, performer, researcher, and maker of maps, zines, books, poetry, short fiction, long fiction, non-fiction, and non-linear, intertextual, hypermedia, and computer-generated narratives. Her pioneering works of digital literature have been exhibited, published, performed, and presented in journals, galleries, museums and festivals around the world. She is a winner of the CBC Quebec Writing Competition, the QWF Carte Blanche Quebec Award, the Expozine Alternative Press Award for Best English Book, the Dot Award for Digital Literature, and the New Media Writing Prize.

luckysoap.com

An Ocean of Static

J.R. Carpenter

Penned in the Margins

LONDON

PUBLISHED BY PENNED IN THE MARGINS
Toynbee Studios, 28 Commercial Street, London E1 6AB
www.pennedinthemargins.co.uk

First published 2018
This edition 2019

Printed in the United Kingdom by CPI Group

ISBN
978-1-908058-46-1

CONTENTS

An Ocean
of Static

The static's like the sound of thinking. Not of any single person thinking, nor even a group thinking, collectively. It's bigger than that, wider — and more direct. It's like the sound of thought itself, its hum and rush.

TOM MCCARTHY, *C*

in memory of Rose Krauss
first daughter across

NOTE TO THE READER

This book is made of other books. The poems in this book are composed of facts, fictions, fragments, and codes collected from accounts of voyages undertaken over the past 2,340 years or so, into the North Atlantic, in search of the Northwest Passage, and beyond, into territories purely imaginary.

These poems are intended to be read on the page and to serve as scripts for the live performance of a body of web-based works. They retain traces of the syntax and grammar of code languages.

LEGEND

// stage direction

#{variable}

['argument']

narrative

    voices

        are separated

            by indentation

        // a voice is followed by a break

Once Upon a Tide

// To be read under cover of
// ['canvas', 'oilskin', 'tarp',
// 'half-light', 'shadow', 'shelter',
// 'fog', 'gloom', 'murk', 'new moon'].

Once upon a ['high', 'spring', 'slack', 'neap'] tide we ['drifted', 'coasted', 'slid', 'slipped', 'tacked'] past a ['bay', 'beach', 'cape', 'cove', 'dune', 'lagoon'], our ship ['brought us hither', 'a brave vessel', 'tight and yar and bravely rigged', 'most strangely landed', 'so near the bottom run'].

On the ['lower', 'main', 'middle', 'poop', 'side', 'quarter'] deck two ['old', 'young', 'slim'] ['friends', 'boatswains', 'sailors'] ['hunched', 'perched', 'crouched', 'sat'] ['mending nets', 'baiting lines', 'spinning yarns', 'twisting tales']. From their ['accents', 'apparel', 'dress', 'gestures', 'looks', 'movements'] I ['guessed', 'gathered', 'suspected', 'assumed'] that ['they', 'both', 'the pair', 'the two of them'] had ['been born', 'come', 'hailed', 'sailed', 'journeyed'] from ['braver', 'better known', 'far', 'fairer', 'gentler'] shores, ['clearly', 'surely', 'obviously'] none so ['barren', 'bleak', 'harsh', 'haunted', 'wicked', 'wild'] as these.

As the bells rang for ['morning', 'forenoon', 'first dog'] watch the ['quieter', 'slighter'] one said:

['We are oppressed with travel.', 'We are all sea-swallowed', 'our garments drenched.', 'The sea mocks our frustrated

search.', 'Every drop of water sears against us.', 'The sea, mounting, dashes the fire out.', 'A thousand furlongs of sea', 'the washing of ten tides.', 'The still-closing waters', 'will shortly fill the reasonable shore.', 'They hoist us to cry to the sea', 'the last of our sea-sorrow.', 'I would have sunk the sea within the earth', 'plunged in the foaming brine', 'the ooze of the salt deep.', 'I shall no more to sea.', 'The sea cannot drown me.', 'I am standing water.']

['One bell', 'Two bells', 'Two bells sounded, a pause, one bell', 'Two bells sounded, a pause, two bells', 'Two bells sounded, a pause, two bells, pause, one bell', 'Two bells sounded, a pause, two bells, pause, two bells', 'Two bells sounded, a pause, two bells, pause, two bells, pause, one bell', 'Two bells, a pause, two bells, pause, two bells, pause, two bells'].

In the ['near', 'middle', 'faint', 'far'] distance the ['bulk', 'hulk', ''ghost', 'shadow', 'vision'] of an island loomed. The ['fairer', 'slower', 'sharper'] one ['leaned', 'gestured', 'peered', 'pointed'] in this direction.

After ['a pause', 'a sigh', 'the bells', 'some time', 'what seemed an eternity] the other replied:

['I am king of this country.', 'This fearful country!', 'I could recover the shore.', 'But is this not near shore?', 'How came we ashore?', 'Unto these yellow sands.', 'Come alive to land.', 'Have you no mouth by land?', 'Here shall I die ashore.', 'Here in this island,', 'We lie in an odd angle, arms in a sad knot.', 'This island will not let you believe certain things.', 'Be not afraid, this island is full of noises.', 'The folly of this island!', 'Most opportune place.']

    isle: '#{isle}',

[['Enter like a water-nymph', 'Enter playing and singing', 'Solemn and strange music', 'Enter several strange shapes', 'Gentle actions of salutation', 'A quaint device', 'Soft music', 'Solemn music', 'Enter divers Spirits in shape of dogs and hounds', 'They sing', 'Song', 'A strange, hollow, and confused noise', 'A noise of hunters heard', 'A cry within', 'A frantic gesture', 'A tempestuous noise of thunder and lightning heard', 'Enter a Shipmaster', 'Enter a boatswain', 'Enter Mariners wet']].

['Come', 'Open your mouth', 'A word', 'O, but one word', 'O, wonder', 'O, defend me', 'Doth thy other mouth call me?', 'Monstrous', 'Mercy', 'Mercy on us', 'Alack, for mercy', 'Fury', 'Silence', 'Why, I said nothing!', 'Ha, ha', 'Oh ho', 'Hark', 'Here', 'A most strange story', 'The story of my life', 'Please you, draw near', 'What cheer?', 'How now?', 'All lost', 'Away'] the ['leaner', 'meaner', 'stronger'] one ['croaked', 'spoke', 'whispered', 'exclaimed']. Would you that soon the ['flush', 'half', 'hurricane'] deck be ['standing', 'drowning', 'drenched'] in ['cold', 'mist', 'magic']?

['The strangeness of this business.', 'These are not natural events.', 'I raised the tempest.', 'I called forth the mutinous winds.', 'I bedimmed the noontide sun.', 'I put the wild waters in this roar.', 'A plague upon this howling!', 'Oh, the dreadful thunderclaps!', 'The fire and cracks of sulphurous roaring.', 'Run upon the sharp wind.', 'wound the wind.', 'a mind to sink', 'It is foul weather in us all.']

'The ['sea sorrow', 'mist', 'tempest'] by that ['island', 'hour', 'tide', 'time', 'watch'] was ['certainly', 'clearly', 'unquestionably'] ['uncommon', 'unnatural', 'unsettled', 'grim'], but was that any ['help', 'use'], that ['kind', 'sort',

'type'] of answer? The ['bizarre', 'awkward', 'odd', 'strange'] ness of their ['speech', 'exchange', 'yarn', 'narration'] put a ['cold', 'heavy', 'helpless', 'listless', 'restless']ness in me. In the ['foul', 'frigid', 'humid', 'heavy', 'salt'] air a ['bolt rope', 'cable', 'cuddy lamp', 'riding light', 'lantern'] ['creaked', 'groaned', 'swayed', 'listed']. Under cover of ['canvas', 'murk', 'shadow', 'shelter'] I ['loitered', 'crouched', 'sat', 'stooped']. Long I ['listened', 'waited', 'watched', 'wondered'] ['closely', 'quietly', 'keenly'].

[['Exit.', 'Exeunt.', 'They vanish.']]

Notes on the Voyage of Owl and Girl

// This is a work of fiction.

// Frequent references to actual events,

// persons, and texts are entirely intentional.

// The Voyage.

An owl and a girl most [adventurous', 'curious', 'studious']
['set out', 'set sail', 'sailed away'] in a [bottle-green',
'beetle-green', 'pea-green'] ['boat', 'sieve', 'skiff', 'vessel']; a
['beautiful', 'shipshape', 'seaworthy'] ['craft', 'raft', 'wooden
shoe'], certainly, though a ['good deal', 'wee bit', 'tad'] too
['small', 'high in the stern'] to suit the two of them. They
took a ['bushel', 'barrel', 'bundle'] of ['honey', 'money']
and an ['almanac', 'astrolabe', 'barometer', 'chronometer']
of dubious ['accuracy', 'origin', 'usefulness']. The owl was
['actually', 'basically', 'simply', 'slightly'] ['home sick',
'sea sick', 'sceptical', 'terrible with directions', 'a nervous
traveller']. The girl sought to gain ['definitive', 'further',
'first-hand'] ['knowledge', 'experience', 'proof'] of ['the
Northwest Passage', 'Ultima Thule', 'a strange phenomena
known as sea lung'].

According to my ['calculations', 'library books', 'test
results'], the girl informed the owl, it's ['six', 'seventeen',
'twenty-seven'] ['leagues', 'knots', 'nights', 'nautical miles']
['due north', 'north', 'northeast'] of here. Her ['mother',
'great-aunt', 'grandmother'] had been among the most

revered of ['authors', 'experts', 'philosophers'] on this topic. But the girl had her own ['life to live', 'line of inquiry', 'ideas', 'theories'].

The owl said, ['Birds of a feather stick together', 'Loose lips sink ships', 'Everywhere we go, there we are'].

How soon he ['drifted', 'floated', 'sailed', 'veered'] off ['topic', 'course', 'track', 'radar']!

According to my ['spyglass', 'sea chart', 'sextant', 'sonar'], we're nearing the edge of our ['our story', 'our journey', 'the earth', 'this narrow sea'], the girl said, but still they sailed ['for a year and a day', 'on through the night', 'on until well past bed time'], ['despite the wet and sea fret', by the light of the silvery moon', 'across the North Atlantic', 'on a river of crystal light', 'into a sea of dew'].

By this time, all the owl's ['magazine subscriptions', 'snack food items', 'phone card credits', 'batteries'] had run out.

Don't ['fret', 'jinx us', 'obsess', 'second-guess'], said the girl most ['ardently', 'rationally', 'seriously']. The ['diaries',

'letters', 'lists', 'ships logs'] she kept constitute the entirety of the ['knowledge', 'evidence', 'proof', 'records', 'traces'] we have left of this ['impossible', 'implausible', 'improbable'] voyage toward ['the edge of the earth', 'the fountain of youth'].

// The notes.

May 7th
departed from Dartmouth

>> on board
>> unmoored
>> unhomed

June 15th
mightily pestered with ice and snow

>> don't fret
>> sea wet
>> mist and haze
>> come inland
>> come hell or high water

>>> uncomfortable
>>> untranslatable

>> come home sick
>> come house wreck

come sea wrack and ruin
strewn ashore

June 29ᵗʰ
no hope of landing

a company of isles
full of fair sounds

       silence
       listen

the sea void of ice
the land untroubled with snow

       an ocean of static
       an ocean of noise

within the sounds we sent our boats

       beeps
       blips

tongue slips
loose lips
sink ships

within the snowy mountains
earth and grass such as our moor
and waste grounds of England

a plant of the borage family
sea lung wart
leaves with an oyster-like flavour

July 17th
we fell upon a most strange quantity of ice

far flung
low slung
sea lung

we supposed it to be land

a frozen tide
a breath suspended

we coasted this mass

> impassable impossible impenetrable
> neither land nor sea nor vapour

our shrouds, ropes, and sails frozen
compassed with ice

August 2nd
much troubled with a fly which is called mosquito

August 15th
here we had great hope of a through passage

> legends warn of rip tides
> shallows
> shoals
> reefs
> ridges
> spits
> bars
> stones

this land is nothing in sight but isles

                                   cracks beneath the surface
                                   hydrothermal vents

August 19th
it began to snow

      wind lift
      spin drift

all night with foul weather

      gale blown
      spray sown
      storm seeds

August 20th
we bare in with the land

                                   avoid a void inked-in
                                   where sea monsters swim

August 28th
in this place we continued

        beware
        be where
        be here
        here be dragons

September 1st
six miles by guess into the country

        into the ether

    this place yieldith
    great store of birds
    at the harbour mouth
    great store of cod

September 6th
purposed to depart

        post date
        press here

press on

presently let slip our cables

September 11th
a fair westnorthwest wind

    spoon drift
    moon lifts

we departed with trust

      questions
      chart answers
      sound fathoms
      compass bearings

shaping our course

        mid-ocean smoke
        a sudden sulphurous odour

October 4th

I have now experience of much
of the northwest part of the world

a column of bubbles
tunnels up from the deep

```
- --- / --- .-. --. .- -. .. --.. . /
.. ... / - --- / .-. . -.-. --- --. -.
.. --.. . --..-- / - --- / -.- -. ---
.-- / - .... .- - / .. -. / .- -. / . -
. -.. .-.. . ... ... / ..- -. -.- -. -
-- .-- -. / .... . .- / - .... . .-. . /
 .. ... / --- -. . / .. ... .-.. .- -.
-.. / ..- .-. --- -. / .-- .... .. -
.-. .... / -.-- --- ..- / .... .- ...-
. / .... . - / ..-. --- --- - / -.... .
..-. --- .-. .
```

There He Was, Gone.

// An on-going conversation in four voices.

Listen.

    It's too early.

Can't you hear something?

    It's only the spring snow over the harbour.

Yes. No, you've got wind in your eyes.

    Tell me then. Where was he lost?

After days on the Atlantic...

Near Burnside...

    Still rowing?

Wait.

               we arrive and we have only just ceased leaving

Listen.

    It's too long ago.

           set sail

Don't you sense this?

    It's only the summer gusts over the swell.

          on home sick

Yes. Only, you've got freezing rain in your sails.

    Tell me then. Where was he found?

          ship shape

After seasons on the ocean...

       we coast along edges

Up near Squid Island...

                    house wreck
Still coasting?
                ledges
Wait.
                legible lines
Listen.
        It's too late.
                    caught in a double bind
                    of writing and erasing
Can't you feel it?
        It's only the November breezes over the waves.
Maybe. No, you've got fog in your hands.
        Tell me then. How was he found?
After months on the surf...
                            steer by star light
By Little Heart's Ease...
        Still searching?
                            dead of night reckoning
Wait.
                we write questions
Listen.
                call answers

It's too much.

Won't you see this?

    keen for replies

It's only the winter showers over the coast.

Yes. Maybe, you've got hail in your boots.

    Tell me then. Why was he found?

        know which way the wind blows

After days on the coast...

    one coastline implies another

Over by Trouty...

    implores a far shore

    Still drifting?

        know where the fish are

Wait.

    sure, we've set foot here before

Listen.

    It's too close to home.

Don't you remember anything?

    horizon line far as eye can see

It's only the autumn rain over the bay.

    islands

    sea

Maybe. Maybe, you've got storms in your hair.

know where the rocks aren't

Tell me then. Where was he lost?

between you and me

After weeks on the swell...

an endless unknown ocean

Over by Eastport...

Still floating?

set sail

Wait.

}).use_frame('listen');

// An epilogue of sorts.

How do we piece together a story like this one?
 A mystery.
The title offers more questions than answers.
 There he was, gone.
Where is there?
Who is he?
Where has he gone?
How is this sentence even possible?
 There he was, not there.
As if 'he' is in two places and in no place,
both at once.
 The once of 'once upon a time.'
This story has to do with time.
This story has to do with place.
 That much is clear.
We take time to look around the story space.
What do we see?
 A corner of a map.
An abstraction of a place too detailed to place.
 Unless the places it names are already familiar.
Is this a local story then?

For locals, between locals…

> If we don't know the answer to this question,
> then we are not local.

We seem to have stumbled upon an on-going
> conversation.

> *Listen.*

A dialogue of sorts.

> *It's too late.*

An argument, even.

One interlocutor instigates.

> *Can't you feel anything?*

The other obfuscates.

> *It's only the spring squalls over the bay.*

All that's not said hangs in a heavy mist.

> A sea fret low over a small fishing boat turned
> broadside to a pack of hump-backed slick black rocks.

This story is fishing inshore.

Close to home.

> *Tell me then.*

> *Where was he found?*

A litany of place names follows.

No answers.

More questions.

Wait.

Listen.

This story keeps shifting.

Slow scrolling lines of poem roll in.

set sail on home sick ship shape house wreck.

What help is that to anyone?

We arrive and we have only just finished leaving.

What use is a poem?

We sift through the fine print,

searching for clues.

GALE WARNING IN EFFECT, Funk Island Bank.

Weather conditions for today's date.

Wind northwest 25 knots diminishing

to west 15 this morning and

to light this afternoon.

Is the disappearance hinted at in the title a recent one?

There he was, gone.

Whoever he was, wherever he went,

this story springs from his absence.

Instructions and Notes Very Necessary and Needful to Be Observed in the Purposed Voyage for Discovery of Cathay Eastwards

// A collaborative essay in three voices.

if the wind does serve
go a seaboard the sands

HOME BAY

stones, mud

set off from thence
note the time diligently

document.getElementById("time")

[today's time, today's date]

turn then your glass
keep continual watch

The bells rang for ['First', 'Middle', 'Morning',
'Forenoon', 'First Dog', 'Second Dog'] Watch.

['1 bell',
'2 bells',
'2 bells, pause, 1 bell',

'2 bells, pause, 2 bells',
'2 bells, pause, 2 bells, pause, 1 bell',
'2 bells, pause, 2 bells, pause, 2 bells',
'2 bells, pause, 2 bells, pause, 2 bells,
          pause, 1 bell',
'2 bells, pause, 2 bells, pause, 2 bells,
          pause, 2 bells']

appoint such course
as you think good.

-1775-

January 1ˢᵗ
we entered the Southern Atlantick Ocean

we landed on Staten Island

the carpenters at work upon a spar

many dread to fall in with land

I am quite impartial

January 14th
an island of ice turned out to be land
wholly covered with snow

    we named an island Bird
    on account of the vast number upon it

there is not a tree or shrub to be seen
big enough to make a tooth-pick

    this isle cannot produce ten thousand
    part of the ice we have seen

either there must be more land
or else ice is formed without it

    after two hours of thick fog
    clear weather gave us a sight
    of 3 or 4 rocky islets

farther I did not intend to go
unless some certain signs
of soon meeting with land

the ice islands which surrounded us
showed a flat even surface

some were two or three miles in circuit

January 31ˢᵗ
the fog cleared away a little

we discovered land ahead

3 rocky islets of considerable height

the outer-most terminated in a lofty peak
like a Sugar Loaf

we named an island Southern Thule

the most southern land yet discovered

February 6ᵗʰ
we set our course North

we were now not in a condition
to undertake great things

this wind seems to conduct us
nearer & nearer to the end
of our career

it was no longer to be doubted
the ice hills had deceived us

Sea ice may be divided into three types thus:

STORIS ['from the Danish word meaning
Large Ice', 'consists of small irregular broken
hummocks', 'frequently weathered into
strange shapes', 'formed in the Arctic Basin',
'scattered by Northwest gales', 'moves North
and Northwestward', 'drifts Southward',
'usually arrives in January', 'generally melts
in July and August', 'has generally melted by
September', 'sets into the fjord', 'seldom
chokes the fjord', 'lies as a tongue off the
coast', 'often extends far out to sea']

WEST ICE ['drifts Southward', 'on the Western side', 'spreads Southeastward ', 'extends Eastward', 'generally extends Eastward', 'consists of closely packed sea ice', 'eroded by the elements', 'subject to variations in wind', 'varies in intensity', 'is normally gone from the coast by March or April', 'may stay until June', 'sometimes never completely clears'].

FAST ICE ['also known as Winter Ice', 'forms during periods of low temperature', 'in coastal in coastal areas and fjords', 'with appreciable thickness in the landlocked fjords,' 'does not form with appreciable thickness on the west coast', 'combines with West Ice to render the coast icebound', 'renders the coast icebound from December to June'].

according as the wind serves
from that time forwards

(if your ship be lose, under sail, a hull)
at the end of every four glasses

(except calm)
sound with your lead.

    The line used for a hand lead ['weighs 28 lbs',
    'is 25 fathoms long'].

    It is possible, by the different feel of the materials
    used to tell what mark is in one's hand in the dark.

        The unmarked depths in fathoms
        are called 'the deeps'.

    Thus, the leadsman calls: ['By the deep eleven, in
    eleven', 'A quarter less six, for five and three-quarters',
    'And a half six, for six and a half'] fathoms.

note what depth you find
and also the ground

if it happen by swiftness
that you cannot get ground

note what depth you
prove you find no ground.

> On ['2nd', '3rd', '4th', '5th', '6th'] February, at
> ['1', '1.30', '3', '3.30', '3.40', '4', '4.30', '5', '6',
> '7', '7.30', '9', '9.30', '10', '11'] ['A.M.', 'P.M.']
> ['ground', 'no ground'] was obtained at ['425',
> '180', '120', '130', '200', '300'] fathoms.

as well outwards
as homewards.

> Take soundings whilst under way.

when you come upon any coast
or find any bank in the sea

use your lead oftener
note the depths into harbours

> Take your place at the forward chain plates.

Secure yourself from falling overboard
by a breast band tied between two shrouds.

keep your dead reckoning
note what way the ship has made

Lean forward against the breast band
to swing your lead in the clear.

Throw your lead as far forward as possible.

how her way has been
through the water.

If hove properly, the line pays out
with a little tension as it passes through the hands.

It 's easy to tell when it has reached the
bottom by the sudden slack felt.

consider the sea.

All that is told of the sea has a fabulous sound to an inhabitant of the land, and all its products have a certain fabulous quality, as if they belonged to another planet, from sea-weed to a sailor's yarn.

note things worth noting.

['carraghean', 'japweek', 'bladder wrack', 'knotted wrack', 'serrated wrack', 'sea lettuce', 'sugar kelp', 'tangle', 'turkey feather alga', 'annual seablite', 'sea lung wort', 'autumn squill', 'common scurby grass', 'eel grass', 'glass wort', 'oysterplant', 'oysterthief', 'oarweed', 'prickly salt wort', 'rock samphire']

the wind
upon what point you find it

bent
          by the steady
the force
          of the running
before the
          steady

soft air of the
        gently
blowing gently
        but steady
wind
        blows steadily
from the southward
        rather freshly
a little
        offshore
wind
        very boisterous
blows
        over
tree branches
        exactly
the damp winds
        rain-
bearing
        sheets of spray
borne
        by the
full force

       of the strong
wind
       very strong
and cold
       piercingly cold
impetuous
       and extremely cold
sheltered
       from the cold
the wind
       was fair
being
       not quite fair

behold
       a gale
of wind
       a heavy gale
of wind
       a furious gale
of wind
       arose this night
delayed

          by successive
gales
          heavy gales
of wind
          unfavourable
winds
          delayed us
blowing a gale
          a gale
of wind
          directly
in our teeth

behold
          a squall
with its rising
          arch
and coming
          fury
the storm
          raged
full
          fury

lulled
       and roared again
through the rigging
       north-west
winds
       prevailing
sirocco-like
       winds
from the parched
       deserts
of the interior
       heaped up
fine sand
       minute
rounded particles
       shells and corals
flying
       along the ground
a strong blast
       cracked in the
wind
       became stagnant
and irregular

in its movements
all still
except
the occasional
flapping of canvas
not even
the wind
not even
a breath of wind
there was no wind
there was no wind
a dead calm
perfectly calm air

what force or strength it is
what sails you bear.

an airfoil-shaped body battens
if the leech has a pronounced roach
boltrope along the luff slid in the mast groove
the corner nearest the mast, the throat

a throat in a sprit
a spar which moves against another
an eye through which to pass a rope

the centre of lateral resistance
balances against the centre of effort
a loose-footed sail attaches to the boom
at the tack and clew
the foot is bounded by the tack

    a jib foot
    lazy jacks
    kicking straps help control twist

tighten the foot of the mainsail
distribute strain over large surfaces
support areas of high stress

    the headsail is hanked by clips to the forestay
    the headboard reinforces the head
    a head cringle

the gaff attaches to the throat and peak
the head runs between the throat and peak
snotters lift the sprit and tighten the peak

     the topping lift attaches to the back stay
     tell tails flutter in the wind
     scandalizing the sail

if you should omit to note these things
I would not have you let slip any longer.

     I possessed two or three articles
     which created unbounded astonishment.

do diligently observe
the latitude

and variation of the compass
when you may be ashore

     In every house I was asked to show the compass,
     and by its aid, together with a map,
     to point out the direction of various places.

the place and places
the time and times.

-2004-

November 28th
set off from Cambridge
on the long journey southwards

    crossed the Southern Ocean
    in calm seas and good weather

do the same when you have sight
of any coast or land

December 9th
arrived amongst hundreds of gentoo penguins

    continued south but soon hit sea-ice

do presently the same
with your sailing compass

how it bears off you
noting your judgement

how far you think it
drawing the form in your book

    the shifting brash ice made fascinating patterns

        ice the consistency of porridge
        impossible to move through

    we reached our limit

        edged slowly out of the pack-ice
        retracing the path we had forged

how it appears to you
how part thereof bears off you

    a disappointed crew returned
    to the edge of the sea-ice

        began the journey northwards

and the extremes also
in sight of the same land at both ends.

travelled north through fantastic scenery

some parts of the coast
quite familiar by now

distinguish by letters
what point of the compass

do you again set
that first land seen

December 17th
endured a plane journey of two and a half hours

December 18th–21st
engaged in training

walking with crampons

walking roped together as a pair

setting up a pulley system

abseiling

ice-axe arrest

breaking a fall

crevasse rescue

camping on a glacier

of the parts there of
that you first observed.

December 22nd
set up the GPS station to run continuously

monitoring small movements
in the earth's crust

if you can well perceive
discern the notable points

December 24th
a pleasant walk along the scree slopes

or signs upon the land
you may then see

there are only two of us staying in this isolated hut
throughout the festive season

only two of us on an island the size of Wales

distinguishing by letters
drawing in your book

we visited a number of survey points
on nearby islands

the shape of the same land
as it appears unto you

the aerial survey kit arrived

    we took low-level photographs
    of penguin colonies

January 2nd
all others have departed
I await the good weather
needed to complete our missions.

and so the third time
in passing any and every coast

    every ['cliff', 'bay', 'beach', 'bight', 'cape', 'cove',
    'delta', 'dune', 'lagoon', 'harbour', 'headland', 'sand
    island', 'rocky islet', 'isthmus', 'peninsula', 'point',
    'ria', 'river estuary', 'mouth', 'stack', 'spit']

draw the manner
of biting in every bay

every harbour or river mouth
the lying out of every point or headland

every ['needle-shaped column', 'steep rock face',
'small island', 'accumulation', 'ridge of sand', 'or
pebbles extending into water', 'just above the
surface', 'shaped by wind', 'jutting into sea']

(unto which you may give apt names
at your pleasure).

Our general named sundry islands

mountains, capes, and harbours

after the names of divers noblemen

and other gentlemen his friends

as well on the one shore

as also on the other.

where high cliffs are
where low land is

whether sand
hills or woods
not omitting
to note

any thing sensible
any good purpose.

   attend to the words of the sovereign birds

      liberate an eagle to carry the soul aloft

   the soul guide is an eagle

      the soul guide is a dove

carefully
with great heed

note observations as aforesaid
and afterwards make demonstration

   I was no bird of passage

no gannet
or albatross

to circle once
and dip a wing

and then fly on over
the boundless ocean.

how far the land you first saw
was then from you

In England any person fond of natural history
enjoys in his walks a great advantage
by always having something
to attract his attention...

how far the one par
from the other

but in these fertile climates

teeming with life

the attractions are so numerous

he is scarcely able to walk at all.

upon what course
one lieth from the other.

an Englishman
        born an Englishman
cultivated in England
        manufactured in England
brought up by Englishmen
        two Englishmen
a number of Englishmen
        from English extraction
English colonists
        English merchants
English miles
        English spurs
English potatoes
        many English plants
behold the English flowers
        common English rain

an English landscape
        an English park
an English rook
        an English mail-coach
an English cottager
        an English vessel
returned to England
        under English colours
property of the English
        to own as English
the English kind
        the English character
the English greyhound
        the English species
in England
        to England
since leaving England
        absence from England
mistaken for England
        appreciated in England
nearer to England
        dearer than in England
decidedly British

the British nation
much too English
our English breed
compared with England
a country church in England
worthy of any road in England
a close resemblance to England
England was brought vividly before my mind

when you come upon any coast
where you find floods and ebbs

note the time of the highest
and lowest water in every place

we made a good run

there are tides which run

slake or still water
off full sea

the tide rose

a strong flood-tide

which way the flood doth run
how the tides do set

above the tidal influence

down to the water's edge

how much water
what force the tide hath

the tide near the head

as the tide falls

to drive a ship in one hour
or in the whole tide

at lower-water spring-tides

of lowest water at spring-tides

what difference
between the running

　　the tides were always wearing

of the flood
and the ebb.

if upon any coast
the current run always one way

note the same duly
what force it hath to drive a ship.

　　She was launched in *1820*.

　　　　　She never saw active service.

as often as you may conveniently
come upon any land

　　Her career as a survey ship began in *1826*.

She was thoroughly prepared for her work.

make observation
for latitude and variation

> Before her second voyage her deck was raised by 18
> inches and her rig was converted from brig to barque
> by the addition of a mizzen mast.

>> The mizzen made her more handy under sail
>> and the raised deck increased the space below.

with your instrument
for trying of distances

> Nevertheless, her crew lived under
> extremely cramped conditions.

>> No fewer than 76 people were aboard
>> when she sailed for South America in *1831*.

observe the platform of the place
and many things (worth noting).

How ['purple', 'fiery', 'swiftly',
'tumultuous'] appeared the clouds.

     They seemed to ['dash against',
     'oppose'] each other.

The skies appeared streaked with ['purple flame',
'blood'] overhead;

     the flaming lightning ['streaming',
     'darting about'] in every direction
     seemed to fill the world with fire,

heavy thunder kept the earth in a constant tremor.

     ['The high forests bent to the blast of',
     'The sturdy limbs of the trees cracked in']
     the wind.

The rain ['came down with such rapidity',
'fell in such quantities'] that every object
was totally obscured,

excepting the continual ['streams',
'rivers'] of lightning pouring from the clouds.

All seemed a frightful chaos.

your whole travel
description of discovery

will be chiefly
at your hands.

TELEPHONE REPORTS OF ACTUAL
WEATHER CONDITIONS AROUND THE
COAST MAY BE OBTAINED FROM:

Sennen 352
Lizard 290444'
Plymouth 42534
Chivelstone 259
Brixham 2156
Seaton 21814
Portland 820 400
Swanage 2146

Freshwater 752265

Fawley 893 574

Niton 730 284'

Shoreham-by-Sea 2226

Pett 3171

Dover 210008

Manston 351, Ext. 220

Shoeburyness 2271 Ext. 476

Frinton-on-Sea 5518

Aldeburgh 2779

Mablethorpe 7747

Gt. Yarmouth 51338

Spurn Point 351

Bridlington 850 203

Whitby 2107

Redcar 474639

North Shields 572691

Coldingham 287

Crail 666

Fraserburgh 3044

Lossiemouth 2121 Ext. 406

Forres 72161 Ext. 674

Portmahomack 210

Wick 2216
Lerwick 2239
Kirkwall 3802
Strathy 210

you may not forget.
note as much as you can.

learn or perceive
the manner of the soil

This place called the Lick lies
between the head of the swamp
and the ascent of the ridge.

The earth, from the surface to an unknown
depth is an almost white tenacious fattish clay
which all kinds of cattle lick into great caves
pursuing the delicious vein.

It is the common opinion of the inhabitants
that this clay is impregnated with saline vapours
arising from fossil salts deep in the earth.

I could discover nothing saline in its taste
but I imagined an insipid sweetness.

Horned cattle, horses, and deer are immoderately
fond of it. Their excrement, which almost totally
covers the earth to some distance round this place,
appears to be perfect clay which when dried by the
sun and air, is almost as hard as brick.

the fruitfulness of every place
and disposition of the people

the commodities they have
what they covet and desire.

The rocks and fossils are of various species including:
['quartz', 'iron', 'flint', 'mica', 'ochre', 'gravel',
'granulated stone'].

There are great piles of a ['porous', 'friable',
'white'] rock in ['large', 'nearly horizontal']
masses, which ['seems to be a heterogeneous
concrete', 'consists of pulverized seashells',

'contains a small proportion of sand', 'is
soft and easily wrought into any form', 'of
sufficient consistence for constructing any
building'].

give trifling things
unto such people

We brought with us:

two red caps, three bracelets, twelve razors, twelve steels
two pounds of nutmeg, twenty of sugar, fifteen of soap
several dozen wooden beads, an excellent substitute for coin
silver coins, buttons, bells, Spanish blankets
quilted caps, knit nightcaps, knit purses
garters and girdles of buff
gloves of all sorts, knit and of leather
shoes of Spanish leather
pewter bottles, flagons, and spoons
combs of horn
handkerchiefs of several colours wrought
fine cloth
linen of divers sorts

spectacles of the common sort
glasses of English making
hour glasses, looking glasses,
looking glasses for women
glazen eyes against the dust
twenty knives, knives in sheaths, knives of good edge
needles of every kind, needles great and small
locks and keys, hinges and bolts
pots of cast iron
rolls of parchment
a large map of London
a map of England set out in fair colours
divers of our country toys

    With our gifts they were
    by no means satisfied.

We underestimated the quality
of goods traded in this part of the world.

    Our paltry gifts were scorned.

We brought away:

a map of their country, a view of their navy
gum and turpentine, tar and pitch
cables and cordage, masts for ships
iron, cotton, hemp, and corn
flax, ivory, gold, and pearls
dried fruits, the fruits of other countries
the seeds of strange herbs, strange flowers
wines and marmalades
sweet oils and sundry delicacies
saffron, fresh salmon
trout and lobster
hides and furs
a black ox
one young man
two of their dogs

offer them courtesy
friendship.

Through the act of looking the ['writer', 'travel writer',
'geographer', 'naturalist', 'survivalist', 'tourist']

['describes', 'objectifies', 'classifies', 'mystifies',
'tells a story of', 'searches for', 'appropriates',
'equates with the desire to possess', 'possesses',
'invents'] ['nature', 'views of pure nature',
'the picturesque', 'the observed', 'the aggression of
imperialism', 'the world', 'the new world', 'a world
whose only history is about to begin', 'other parts
of the world as having no history', 'optical and
semiotic imagery in a mirror dance of colonial
mirror-making', 'a type of counter discourse',
'subordinated or marginal groups', 'native people',

> 'rhetorical, stylistic and discursive practices
> that encode ideology', 'a rhetoric to enable
> colonization', 'a dominant or metropolitan
> culture'].

you may
win their love.

They are very simple in all their conversation,
marvellously thievish, especially for iron, inscrutable,
incomprehensible, strong and nimble, naked and

scarcely protected from this tempestuous climate.

They eat all their meat raw, eat fish raw, just
as they take them from the water, eat grass
and ice with delight.

They drink salt water.

They live mostly on fish, in the nature of
fishes, by hunting all the winter, by diving for
shells at lower-water spring-tides.

They believe that when they die
they descend on the horizon

like stars.

They dye their faces black with brayed charcoal,
cover their faces with grease thick as a knife blade,
mark their ribs and thighs and faces with a white
pigment, do not suffer with shame or pain beyond
the present moment, hold their spears quivering in
their grasp ready to hurl.

The women come out with heads downcast,
swing their shoulders with a force that would
tire an ordinary person, wear purple threaded
with cowries falling to their breast.

They never cease war.

The women are witches, filled with the power
of the fetish extremely clamorous, painted in
various ways, all dressed alike.

They lack manners and decency.

The women have many enchantments,
hair plaited in more than one hundred tresses,
tusks as long as those of wild boar.

They have skill in wrestling, good stature, slender
hands and feet, broad visages, small eyes, and wide
mouths, huts made from fishes' backbones.

The women climb trees with facility.

They sleep on the wet ground coiled up like animals.

The women are not themselves.

They pronounce their language deep in the throat.

The women can no longer speak.

favour toward you
not any wrong or hurt.

~1578~

May 31ˢᵗ
departed from Harwich

      fourteen days without sight of any land
      or any other living thing

June 20ᵗʰ
the general descried land
and found it to be West Friesland

the savage and simple people
so soon as they perceived us
fled fearfully away

we brought away two of their dogs

we left in recompense bells, looking glasses
and diverse of our country toys

June 23rd
having a fair and large wind
we departed from thence

to the northwards of this coast
we met with much driving ice

June 30th
struck a great whale with such a blow
that the ship stood still

forced to stem and strike
great rocks of ice
and so, as it were,
to make through mighty mountains

July 2ⁿᵈ

a sudden and terrible tempest at the southeast
blowing from the main sea

> upon our backs great countries of ice
> outrageous winds, fleeting islands

July 8ᵗʰ

a more favourable wind at the west northwest
gave us liberty, scope, and sea room

> (great comfort)

plied off to seaward

> resolved there to abide
> until sun might consume
> the ice from the place of our passage

July 10ᵗʰ

the weather continuing thick and dark

> dark mists, continual fog and ice

we should have perished for lack of food to eat

    we should have been eaten by ravenous
    bloody, and men-eating people

July 23rd
a long time now alone

    ice choked up the passage

July 26th
the ship leaky, the stem beaten
much ado to keep above water

    it was the most impossible thing of the world

July 27th
there fell so much snow
with such bitter cold air
that we could scarce see one another
nor handle our ropes and sails
    the winter must be extreme

    where found so unseasonable a summer

July 31ˢᵗ
not withstanding the great storm
with incredible pain and peril
at length got through the ice

      recovered our long wished port
      after many attempts
      and came to anchor

August 9ᵗʰ
after due examination
and true account taken
there was found want of drink and fuel

      it was fully agreed upon
      that no habitation should be there this year

August 30ᵗʰ
the better to allure those brutish and uncivil people
to courtesy against other times of our coming, we left
pictures of men and women in lead, men on
horseback, looking glasses, whistles, and pipes

buried the timber of our pretended fort

sowed pease, corn, and other grain to prove
the fruitfulness of the soil against the next year

dark foggy mists, continual falling snow
and stormy weather

now daily ever more increased

argument of the winter's drawing near

*August 31*th
the taking in of fresh water

*September 1*st
departed from the Sound

*October 1*st
arrived safely in England

there died in all this voyage
not above forty persons

which number is not great

considering

you should be offered wrong
yet not revenge the same lightly.

deal wisely.
keep out of dangers.

We ate
a steady diet
of skins and oil.

We ate one caribou ham
eight bear-paws
and five Canada jays.

We ate the antlers and back bone of a deer
which had been killed in the summer
which wolves and birds of prey had picked clean.

We ate a quantity of spinal marrow
which, although putrid,
was esteemed a valuable prize.

We ate a few morsels of burnt leather
whatever scraps of leather we had
to strengthen our stomachs.

We ate tripe de roche
rock tripe on occasion of isolation
to stave off starvation.

We ate the remains of our shoes
our snow-shoe lashings
several fathoms of raw-hide thongs.

Fresh rawhide reminds one
of pig's feet
if well boiled.

return home again.

adventures with you
our whole country.

Tout le reste est inconnu.

Ten Short Talks About Islands... and by Islands I Mean Paragraphs

// Preface.

Flocks of books open and close, winging their way web-ward. A reader is cast adrift in a sea of white space veined blue by lines of longitude, of latitude, of graph, of paper. The horizon extends far beyond the bounds of the browser window, to the north, south, east and west. Navigating this space (with track pad, touch screen, mouse, or arrow keys) reveals that this sea is dotted with islands… and by islands I mean fluid paragraphs continuously recomposed by JavaScript variables calling words and phrases collected from a vast literary corpus.

Individually, each of these textual islands represents a topic – from the Greek *topos*, meaning place. Collectively they constitute a topographical map of a sustained practice of reading and re-reading and writing and re-writing on the topic of islands. In this constantly shifting sea of variable texts a reader will never wash ashore on the same island twice… and by islands, I really do mean paragraphs.

I. Topical Islands

Islands are ['places that have become commonplaces', 'perfect topics', 'literal metaphors', 'possible only in literature']. Topical islands are ['figures of radical isolation', 'off the map', 'off the chart', 'always virgin', 'blind spots on the surface of the known', 'shrouded in obscurity', 'isolated in the present', 'silent', beyond time', 'in a time zone of their own']. They are paragraphs. They ['separate the narrative body from the referential mainland', 'separate the text from the writer's desk', 'separate the text from the reader's finger's', 'surround and enclose the text', 'create their own context']. They are ['textual shores', 'marginal', 'not part of the central body of the text', 'a physical space on the page', 'engulfed in a textual sea'].

II. Soundings

On the ['2nd', '3rd', '4th', '5th', '6th'] February, at ['1', '1.30', '3', '3.30', '3.40', '4', '4.30', '5', '6', '7', '7.30', '9', '9.30', '10', '11'] ['AM', 'PM'] the ship ['proceeded under sail towards', 'was unable to prosecute the search for', 'was unable to make much progress toward', 'wore and stood to the southward, with the intention of getting into the parallel of', 'was on the supposed parallel of', 'bore up for the supposed position of'] Heard Island. ['Bottom', 'No bottom'] was obtained at ['80', '120', '130', '200', '300', '425'] fathoms. It was deemed imprudent to proceed further, ['because of the rocky, uneven nature of the bottom', 'because it is no unusual thing for icebergs to be seen in the locality', 'on account of the uncertain position of the island', 'as coal could not be afforded for steaming', 'as the ship was surrounded by Penguins, uttering their discordant cry'].

III. Measures

This island measures [75, 42, 25, a little over 23, nearly 15, 13.5, just 12, only 11, approximately 9, 5, just over 4, 3, 2.5, roughly 2, half a] km from North to South and [40, 20, over 7, 6, from 1 to 6, 5, 4, 3, 2, under 2, one-and-a-quarter, 1] km from East to West.

IV. Testimonials

Such persons as have travelled to this island do testify that they have found these things following: Of metals: ['gold', 'silver', 'copper', 'lead', 'tin']. Of stones: ['turquoise', 'rubies', 'marble of diverse kinds', 'pearls great and fair', 'jasper', 'crystal']. Of trees: ['cedars', 'firs', 'poplar', 'palms yielding sweet wines', 'sundry strange trees', 'trees to us unknown']. Of fruits: ['figs', 'prunes', 'dates, great', 'raisins, great and small', 'pepper', 'almonds', 'citrons']. Of birds: ['bitters', 'curlews', 'cranes', 'mallards', 'wild geese', 'parrots', 'partridges', 'penguins']. Of beasts for furs: ['martens', 'beavers', 'foxes, black', 'foxes, white', 'leopards']. Of fishes: ['cod', 'salmon', 'seals', 'herrings']. Of worms: silk worms great and large. Of sundry other commodities: ['rosin', 'pitch', 'tar', 'turpentine', 'frankincense', 'honey', 'wax', 'rhubarb', 'olive oil', 'musk', 'salt', 'hemp', 'flax', 'feathers of sundry sorts', 'feathers for pleasure', 'feathers for filling of beds'].

V. Thule

An island ['was sighted', 'was celebrated', 'to the west', 'as yet lies hidden'], lies ['a voyage of five days and nights north', 'a six days' sail north, and near the frozen sea']. ['The climate here is objectionable, with its frequent rains and mists', 'winds, storms and swirling tides', 'exposed on all sides', 'The sun does not set and rise, but simply passes along the horizon', 'The end of the earth, being flat, casts low shadows and cannot raise the darkness to any height', 'there is almost no night', 'under shining night the sun's wheel burns with continuous tinder']. ['The northern parts of our kingdom, the Romans despised', 'Farther North', 'in the extreme North', 'suddenly to the North', 'the farthest island of the ocean', 'set farthest North']. ['The sea is sluggish and heavy to the oar', 'sluggish and solid, 'scarcely penetrable by ships', 'a sea the colour of lead, a sky the colour of smoke', ' There is no proper land nor sea nor air, but a sort of mixture of all three of the consistency of a jellyfish in which one can neither walk nor sail'].

VI. A New Example

This island ['is indeed a very splendid island', 'a little smaller than Iceland', 'irrigated by four pleasant streams', 'endowed with all things necessary for the easy sustenance of human life', 'ruled over by a king who lives in a populous city', 'who keeps his household interpreters skilled in many tongues', 'has a library containing various books in Latin', 'has scarcely two people who understand Latin']. The islanders ['are very ingenious', 'apply themselves to all the skills of the artificer', 'almost as well as we do', 'have a language of their own', 'write with their own characters', 'have mines of all metals', 'are especially rich in gold', 'collect in Greenland skins', 'carry sulphur home in their ships']. Concerning ['this wonderful new example of an island in the northern regions', 'many other islands which no one has yet named', 'which no one has yet given a published description of their situation', 'a multitude of other matters', 'the surveying of navigation of the coasts of the whole world'] a full account is being ['undertaken', 'written lately in a large book', 'in our vulgar tongue'].

VII. Deserted Islands

Geographers say there are two kinds of islands. Continental islands are ['born of disarticulation', 'born of fracture', 'accidental', derived', 'survive the absorption of what once contained them']. Oceanic islands ['rise slowly', 'disappear and then return', 'leave us no time to annex them', 'like eggs, eggs of the sea']. Dreaming of islands is dreaming of ['pure consciousness', 'pulling away', 'starting from scratch', 'beginning anew']. Every island is, in theory, deserted. The deserted island ['is as deserted as the ocean around it', 'may be a desert, but not necessarily', 'doesn't stop being deserted simply because it is inhabited', 'imagines and reflects itself', 'is imaginary']. It is at this very moment literature begins. Literature is ['the attempt to interpret myths at the moment we no longer understand them', 'the mythical recreation of the world', 'painstakingly applied', 'a double without consistency', 'the reconstitution of everyday life', 'separated from the real']. One can hardly imagine a more boring novel.

VIII. *Concrete Island*

The island ['pointed towards the west and the declining sun', 'was sealed off from the world around it', 'was moving back in time to an earlier and more violent period', 'dated, in parts, from before World War II', 'appeared covered by a dense and luxuriant growth', 'and its green swaying ocean']. The grass ['grew waist-high', 'festered over the ground', 'rose and fell like the waves of a brisk sea', 'weaved and turned, moving in endless waves', 'opened a dozen pathways', 'opened and closed as if admitting a large and watchful creature to its green preserve', 'swayed in the night air', 'seethed in the light wind', 'seethed in the night wind', 'seethed and whirled, as if sections of wilderness were speaking to each other', 'rustled excitedly', 'swayed reassuringly', 'flashed with an electric light', 'jostled on all sides like a hostile crowd', 'was a vital medium', 'was silent now', 'was quiet', 'barely moved', 'covered all traces', 'was over four feet deep'].

IX. Crusoe in the Galapagos

My island ['- my brain bred island', '- a little world within itself', 'rose with a tame and rounded outline', '- caught on the horizon like a fly', 'smelled of goat and guano', 'seemed to be a sort of cloud-dump', 'seemed to have been permeated, like a sieve, by subterranean vapours', '- free to a remarkable degree from gales of wind']. My island had one kind of everything: ['one tree snail crept over everything', 'one variety of tree, a sooty, scrub affair', 'one kind of berry, a dark red', 'the goats were white, so were the gulls', 'when all the gulls flew up at once, they sounded like a big tree in a strong wind', 'the whole northern part miserably sterile', 'the whole lower region covered by nearly leafless bushes', 'such wretched-looking little weeds', 'the rocks on the coast abounded with great black lizards', 'a mouse, a rat distinct from the common kind', 'a most singular group of finches', 'one small lizard', 'one snake, which was numerous', 'thousands of huge tortoises', 'of toads and frogs there are none']. ['The hissing, ambulating turtles got on my nerves', 'I did not see one beautiful flower', 'Even the bushes smelt unpleasantly', 'I often gave way to self-pity.', 'Do I deserve this? 'Was there a moment when I

actually chose this?', 'I didn't know enough.', 'Why didn't I know enough of something?', 'The books I'd read were full of blanks', 'Although I diligently tried to collect as many plants as possible, I succeeded in getting very few', 'I did not pay sufficient attention', 'None of the books has ever got it right'].

X. Castaway

['I was a bottle bobbing on the waves with a scrap of writing inside', 'I was carried by the waves', 'Through the hours of despair on the waves', 'The the roar of the waves', 'The wind and wave-roar', 'The waves picked me up and cast me ashore']. I am ['cast away', 'a castaway', 'indeed cast away', 'not a bird of passage', 'not a prisoner', 'not a story', 'not persuaded', 'unknown to myself', 'wondering how I come to be here', 'saved', 'on an island yet', 'alone on the waves', 'alone', 'all alone', 'a woman alone', 'a woman cast ashore', 'a woman washed ashore', 'a free woman', 'now a madwoman', 'waiting for the book to be written that will set me free'].

TRANS.MISSION [A.DIALOGUE]

'Begin Transmission.'; +choose(w) +'?'; 'With a ' +choose(question) + '
+' ' +choose(weather) +' on the ' +choose(water) +'.'; choose(distant) +
choose(havent) +' the ' +choose(necessary) +' ' +choose(cases) +' been
' +choose(hisher) +' '+choose(condolence) +'s.'; 'Why '+choose(cant) +' tl
+'?'; choose(wethey)+' '+choose(waited)+' '+choose(numbers)
the '+choose(stories) +'s seem to ' +choose(say) +'.'; choose(w) +' d
'+choose(information)+' '+choose(of) +' ' +choose(past) +' '+choose(passag
+' ' +choose(hear) +' these ' +choose(strange) +' ' +choose(sound) +'s.
+choose(know) +' this ' +choose(landscape)+'?'; 'The ' +choose(passage)
' +choose(are) +' ' +choose(conditions) +'.'; 'Receiving ' +choose(shining)
the '+choose(water) +' in ' +choose(weather) +' like this?'; choose(amoun
+choose(are) +' '+choose(prepared) +'.'; choose(might) +' '+choose(travelle
choose(past) +' '+choose(traveller)+'s '+choose(wrote)+' '+choose(maps)+'.
' +choose(wethey) +' ' +choose(always) +' seem to ' +choose(leave) +'
+' ' +choose(network) +'s take ' +choose(time) +' to ' +choose(say)
+choose(wethey) +' '+choose(communicated) +'?'; choose(condolence +
+' have been ' +choose(sign) +'s. '; choose(strange) +' ' +choose(sound) +'
' +choose(receiving) +'...'; 'Did ' +choose(you) +' ' +choose(hear) +' th
+choose(communicated) +'.'; 'One ' +choose(traveller) +' ' +choose(beckor
' +choose(might) +' ' +choose(heshe) +' ' +choose(say) +'?'; choose(novelis
+choose(landscape) +'s ' +choose(always) +' ' +choose(start) +' from these
+'s\' ' +choose(relative) +'s ' +choose(need) +' ' +choose(more) +'
by'+choose(season)+''+choose(amount)+''+choose(maps)+''+choose(migh
' +choose(horizon) +' ' +choose(wrote) +'?'; 'The ' +choose(proximity) +'
'In these ' +choose(strange) +' '+choose(maps) +', the ' +choose(water)
+choose(say) +' '+ choose(past) +' ' +choose(question) +'s?'; choose(sign) +'
+choose(screen) +'.'; 'Is the ' +choose(network) +' ' +choose(working) +'?
'Please try again.'; main.appendChild(last); function produce_stories()

/hat ' +choose(start) +'s from a ' +choose(question) + '?'; choose(season)

hoose(landscape) +'s, to ' +choose(beckon) +' ' +choose(usthem) +'.';

·hoose(prepared)+' yet?'; 'The '+choose(operator)+' '+choose(transmit)+'s

-choose(traveller)+'s ' +choose(need)+' '+choose(more)+' '+choose(tickets)

choose(time) +'.'; choose(provisions) +' ' +choose(ranlow)+', or so

·e '+choose(operator)+' ' +choose(transmit)+' '+choose(hisher)+'

s?'; 'The ' +choose(transatlantic) +' ' +choose(network) +' '+choose(cant)

·oose(might) +' the ' +choose(operator) +' ' +choose(now) +' come to '

·m ' +choose(place)+' '+choose(proved) +' '+choose(harsh) +'.'; 'Conditions

choose(static) +', '+choose(receiving)+'...'; 'Who can '+choose(know)+'

' +choose(part) +'s of the '+choose(novelist) +'\'s '+choose(stories) +' '

s ' +choose(now) +' ' +choose(leave) + ' these ' +choose(landscape) +'s?';

:hoose(numbers) +' were from '+choose(place) +'.'; choose(w)+' is it that

:hoose(part) +'s from the ' +choose(information)+'?'; choose(transatlantic)

·e ' +choose(necessary) +' ' +choose(stories) +'s.'; choose(havent) +' '

·ere ' +choose(sent) +' ' +choose(time) +' ago. '; 'There ' +choose(might)

+choose(static) +' on the ' +choose(screen) +'.'; 'A ' +choose(sound) +',

+choose(sound) +'?'; choose(distant) +' ' +choose(network) +'s have '

s the ' +choose(operator) +'.'; 'Which words of ' +choose(condolence) +'

\'s ' +choose(stories) +'s ' +choose(of) +' ' +choose(distant) +' '

:hoose(horizon) +'s.'; choose(might)+' '+choose(past)+' '+choose(traveller)

:hoose(information) +' from '+choose(usthem)+'?'; choose(possibly) +', but

·be ' +choose(wrong) +'.'; choose(w) +' was the ' +choose(proximity) +'

:hoose(landscape) +'s ' +choose(resemble) +' those of '+choose(place)+'.';

' +choose(always)+' ' +choose(shining)+'.'; choose(but) +'... does that '

f ' +choose(distant) +' ' +choose(weather) +' ' +choose(start) +' on the '

·oose(wethey) +' ' +choose(suspect) +' it\'s ' +choose(working) +'.';

Etheric Ocean

// An underwater soundscape in two voices.

this sea is nothing in sight but isles.....................................

I'll ['wade in', 'wait', 'wait a while'].
I'll ['walk in', 'walk away', 'walk on water'].
I'll ['want'], I'll ['warble'], I'll ['warrant'].
I'll ['wash', 'wash up', 'wash ashore'].
I'll ['waste land', 'waste water', 'waste paper'].

> reflected

I'll ['water', 'down', 'fall', 'front', 'log', 'mark', 'meadow'].
I'll ['weave', 'web', 'wave', 'waver'].
I'll ['wave you over'].
I'll ['weep', 'weigh in', 'weigh anchor'].
I'll ['weaken', 'wean', 'wear', 'weather', 'warn', 'proof'].
I'll ['weather this storm'].

> refracted

['weird']. ['welcome']. ['watch'].

[what will you do]

I'll ['west', 'wet', 'whack', 'wharf', 'while away', 'whimper'].

I'll ['whine'], I'll ['whinge'], I'll ['whirl', 'wind', 'pool'].

I'll ['whisk', 'whiskey', 'white flag', 'white lie', 'light',
    'wash', 'water', 'great white whale'].

I'll ['whisper']. I'll ['whistle'].

I'll ['whoop', 'whoosh', 'whorl', 'wide open', 'wild',
    'wilful'].

I'll ['win'], I'll ['wing'], I'll ['wind'].

['wink', 'winnow', 'winter', 'wire', 'wisen', 'wise crack',
    'wish'].

I'll ['with draw', 'with hold', 'with stand'].

I'll ['witness', 'wonder', 'word', 'work'].

I'll ['worry', 'worsen', 'worship'].

I'll ['wound']. I'll ['wow']. I'll ['wonder'].

I'll ['write up', 'write down', 'write off', 'write out',
    'write away'].

I'll ['wrong']. ['wrong number'].

a company of isles...

all communications should be addressed to the company

full of fair sounds...

If you can't hear sound here, it's possible that your computer or browser doesn't support the file format. Or, If you can't hear sound here, it's possible that your computer or browser doesn't support the file format. Or, If you can't hear sound here, it's possible that your computer or browser doesn't support the file format. Or, If you can't hear sound here, it's possible that your computer or browser doesn't support the file format. Or, If you can't hear sound here, it's possible that your computer or browser doesn't support the file format. Or, If you can't hear sound here, it's possible that your computer or browser doesn't support the file format. Or, If you can't hear sound here, it's possible that your computer or browser doesn't support the file format. Or, If you can't hear sound here, it's possible that your computer or browser doesn't support the file format. Or, If you can't hear sound here, it's possible that your computer or browser doesn't support the file format. Or, If you can't hear sound here, it's possible that your computer or browser doesn't support the file format. Or, If you can't hear sound here, it's possible that your computer or browser doesn't support the file format. Or, If you can't hear sound here, it's possible that your computer or browser doesn't support the file format. Or, If you can't hear sound here, it's

possible that your computer or browser doesn't support the file format. Or, If you can't hear sound here, it's possible that your computer or browser doesn't support the file format. Or, that you have your speakers turned off. that you have your speakers turned off.that you have your speakers turned off. that you have your speakers turned off.that you have your speakers turned off.that you have your speakers turned off. that you have your speakers turned off.that you have your speakers turned off.that you have your speakers turned off. that you have your speakers turned off.that you have your speakers turned off.that you have your speakers turned off. that you have your speakers turned off. that you have your speakers turned off.that you have your speakers turned off.that you have your speakers turned off.that you have your speakers turned off.that you have your speakers turned off. that you have your speakers turned off.that you have your speakers turned off.that you have your speakers turned off. Or, that you are a land mammal bending ear to hear sounds deep Or, that you are a land mammal bending ear to hear sounds deep Or, that you are a land mammal bending ear to hear sounds deep Or, that you are a land mammal bending ear to hear sounds

deep Or, that you are a land mammal bending ear to hear sounds deep Or, that you are a land

mammal bending ear to hear sounds deep Or, that you are a land mammal bending ear to hear sounds deep Or, that you are a land mammal bending ear to hear sounds deep Or, that you are a land mammal bending ear to hear sounds deep Or, that you are a land mammal bending ear to hear sounds deep Or, that you are a land mammal bending ear to hear sounds deep Or, that you are a land mammal bending ear to hear sounds deep Or, that you are a land mammal bending ear to hear sounds deep Or, that you are a land mammal bending ear to hear sounds deep Or, that you are a land mammal bending ear to hear sounds deep Or, that you are a land mammal bending ear to hear sounds deep Or, that you are a land mammal bending ear to hear sounds deep Or, that you are a land mammal bending ear to hear sounds deep Or, that you are a land mammal bending ear to hear sounds deep under water.under water.under water. under water. under water. under water.under water. under

into the ether...

Either ether or ['a colourless, highly volatile, flammable liquid', 'an aromatic odour and sweet, burning taste',

'a solvent', 'an inhalant', 'the clear sky', 'the heavens', 'a hypothetical substance', 'postulated to account for the propagation of electromagnetic radiation', 'the medium supposed by the ancients to fill the upper regions of space']

an etheric ocean...

Through its early association with ['shipping', 'the sea', 'distant lands'], wireless evoked ['a slight apprehension over the depthless void', 'the wonders of distant communication that'] technology had revealed to the world.

['This watery planet can still keep secrets from us',

The ether ['was its own ocean'].

'The ocean is a noisy place',

The ether ['was at once vast and diffuse'].

'When humans first heard whales singing,
they believed they were listening to ghosts',

The ether ['beckoned explorers to navigate
its unfathomable depths'].

'Marconi believed his radio signals might pick up
the sounds of sailors drowned in the Atlantic',

Drifting through the spectrum in search of transmissions
from the most distant points around the globe was a
journey traversed primarily across mysterious expanses ['of
silence']...

'Marconi spent his last years trying to establish
contact between this world and the next'].

...mysterious expanses ['of static'].

an ocean of static...

Static is like the sound of thinking.

['Not of any single person thinking',
'Not of a group thinking, collectively'].

['It's bigger than that', 'It's wider than that — and more direct', 'It's like the sound of thought itself, its hum and rush'].

Each night it ['recoils with a wail', 'rolls back in crackling waves', 'carries her away, all rudderless'], until her finger, nudging at the ['dial', 'pencil', 'pen', 'cursor'], can get some traction on it all, some sort of leeway.

The first stretches are always ['angry', 'plaintive', 'sad', 'mute'].

Hunched over the ['console', 'synthesiser', 'instrument', 'mechanism'], ['among fraying cords and soldered wires', 'her breathing an extension of the frequency of the air she's riding on'], she gets the first quiet clicks.

Words start forming: ['she jots down the signals as straight graphic lines, long ones and short ones', 'she begins to transcribe curling letters'], dim and grainy in the arc-light of her desktop.

[a s l o w / p u r p o s e f u l / u n f o l d i n g o f s o u n d]

If you look —
through the window, through the night

Noise ['ripples through the listener'],

ripples of light break over their bodies —
blue and white —
like waves in the wake of a swimmer...

['a semantic survival'].

...long laps of legs kicking and endless reaching arms.

an ocean of silence...

Distance ['distracts', 'distorts', 'distends'].
The ['heart', 'head', 'ear'] hears
what it ['wishes', 'wants', 'needs'] to.

Noise ['is not silence's opposite'].

No, noise ['is, in a way, the double of silence'].

an ocean of noise...

Noise ['is a thick and tactile curtain', 'a temporal fabric'].

Noise ['obliquely approaches
the irregular fabric of sounding'].

Noise ['fluctuates through any given present', 'presents no
discernible figure of meaning', 'has no meaning', 'distributes
sound as non-meaning', 'the non-knowledge of meaning',
'non-identity'].

Noise ['exceeds its own identity', 'suspends itself'].

What I am calling noise ['is an outside, mutating term',
'outside the range of rational signification',
'below the spectrum of recognition'].

What I am calling noise ['does not function outside
time', 'does not cohere with the figural self-identity of
meaning', 'does not fold'].

An ocean of noise ['is a gathered density of inconspicuous perceptions', 'composed of tiny sub-cognitive movements', 'the fluctuating milieu of dailiness', 'the obscure relation within the ordinary', 'the habitual'].

An ocean of noise ['signifies an excess', 'time's excess', 'unwilled surplus', 'the by-product of economies', 'the extreme of difference'].

Noise ['is inefficient', 'pollutant', 'the present', 'a confusion of figure and field'].

Noise ['belongs to poverty'].

Noise ['is made'].

This is the Certified Track of S.S. Philadelphia American Line Showing Points Where Mr. G. Marconi Received Messages From Cornwall, England, by Wireless Telegraphy.

you know what I wonder about is what those who were on board this ship spoke about – amongst themselves, between themselves...

shores between in receiving and sending
between in signals between in messages
between in hours off

off the record during the off hours
in between messages

the during record the off themselves
between themselves
amongst about

in between signals
in between sending and receiving

spoke ship this board on were
who those what is about wonder

in between shores between in receiving and sending
between in signals between in messages

I what know you know what I wonder about
is what those who were on board this ship spoke about

between in hours off the during record
the off themselves between themselves

                amongst themselves between themselves

amongst about spoke ship

                off the record during the off hours
                      in between messages

this board on were who those what is

                      in between signals
                in between sending and receiving

about wonder I what know you
in between shores

Along the Briny Beach

// A walk in two voices:
// Walrus and Carpenter

Watching a coast as it slips by the ship is like thinking about an enigma.

Far shore highlights the tide.
White cliff writes the gulf.
     drift along the storied memory —

There it is before you — smiling, frowning, inviting, grand, mean, insipid (or savage) — with an air of whispering *Come and find out.*

Ship explains the harbours.

Expedition up the River.

Peninsulas pronounce the cold water.

Immense streams of basaltic lava.

     track along the fabled wind-loud uncharted—

Fragments not transported by the river.

Sediments highlight the storm surge.

Excavation of the valley.

Brines abandon.

Condor, habits of.

Spit reveals the high tide.

Erratic boulders of great size.

        wander along the salt-glittering
        wave-washed —

Return to the ship.

    Ports reveal the undercurrent.
    Breezes fog.
    Coastal ranges wreck.
    Peninsula prints the wave.
        range along the distant waiting line —

The coast was almost featureless, as if still in the making, with an aspect of monotonous grimness. Everything was withdrawn as far as possible, indrawn: the tide far out, the ocean shrunken, seabirds in ones or twos.

Tucutuco.
Molothrus, cuckoo-like habits.
Tyrant-flycatcher.
Mocking-bird.
Carrion Hawks.
Flamingos.
Sacred Tree.
Sand Dunes.
Saline incrustations.

The rackety, icy, offshore wind disrupted the formation of a lone flight of Canada geese.

Scissor-beak.
Kingfisher.
Parrot,
and Scissor-tail.

No birds were flying overhead—
There were no birds to fly.

   Penguin.
   Geese.
   Eggs of Doris.

The edge of a colossal jungle so dark-green as to be almost
black ran straight, like a ruled line far, far away along a
blue sea whose glitter was blurred by a creeping mist.

   Blue Haze.

Peninsula inscribes the gulf.

   Heavy Rain.

Sea creatures conceal.

   Musical Frogs.

Capes archive the mists.

Phosphorescent insects.

       track along the distant waiting unnamed—

Noise made by a Butterfly.

       Moorings reveal the deep waters.

Entomology.

       Sandstone cliffs chart the harbours.

Ants.

       come and go along the uncharted edge—

The sky was darker than the sea.
The sea was the colour of mutton-fat jade.

       The sun came out for a minute.

The sun was shining on the sea, shining with all its might
and this was odd, because it was the middle of the night.

The sun was fierce.
The land seemed to glisten
and drip with steam.

Great Evaporation.
Singular Incrustations.
Burnished Rocks.
Rocks, non-volcanic.
Causes of discoloured Sea.

The oily and languid sea.
The uniform sombreness of the coast
seemed to keep me away from the truth of things.

Differences in the species on different islands.
Tameness of the birds.
Fear of man an acquired instinct.

Coastline daydreams the canals.

Boats anchor the oceans.

Coral reefs encode.

Sandstone investigates the sea.

Breakwaters articulate the sea creature.

lap along the briny—

drift along the briny distant waiting—

Boats explain the waves.

Sands scan the tidal river.

Outports wash.

Sand bar highlights the undercurrent.

Coastal range navigates the waves.

storm along the wave-washed wind-loud—

lap along the fabled salt-glittering in-between space—

It was cold and windy

scarcely the day to take a walk
on that long beach.

O Oysters, come and walk with us!
A pleasant walk, a pleasant talk
along the briny beach.

The wind numbed our faces
blew back the low rollers.

The sea black and boiling.
Stones twisted round.
Great Wave.
Volcanic phenomena.
Elevatory and eruptive forces.
Cause of earthquakes.
Slow elevation of mountain-chains.

Along the wet sand in rubber boots
we followed a track of big dog-prints.

We were walking close at hand.
We wept like anything to see such quantities of sand.

If this were only cleared away, it would be grand!

If seven maids with seven mops swept it for half a
year, do you suppose that they could get it clear?

I doubt it.

Topical island frames the delta.
Far shores blow.
Sandstones pilot the ripple.
progress along the briny salt-glittering
shore—

The sea was wet as wet could be, the sands were dry as dry.
You could not see a cloud, because no cloud was in the sky.

We walked on a mile or so
and then rested on a rock conveniently low.
All the little Oysters stood and waited in a row.

I wanted to get as far as my proto-dream-house
my crypto-dream-house

The time has come to talk of many things:
Of shoes and ships and sealing-wax,
of cabbages and kings,
and why the sea is boiling hot,
and whether pigs have wings.

(Many things about this place are dubious.)

Numerous gigantic extinct Quadrupeds.

Recent Extinction.
Fossils.
Two Species of Ostrich.
Habits of Oven-bird.
Armadillos.
Venomous Snake, Toad, Lizard.

Coastline coordinates the channel.

Hibernation of Animals.

Dockyards carve.

Habits of Sea-Pen.

Squalls blur.

Antiquarian Relic.

hike along the wind-loud in-between space—

The voice of the surf heard now and then was a positive
pleasure, like the speech of a brother.

Coasts draw the tidal wave.

It was something natural,

Eastern coasts drain.

that had its reason,

Atolls eliminate.

that had a meaning.

Sandstones record the maelstroms.

meander along the waiting uncharted ledge—

I listened, I listened for the sentence, for the word, that
would give me the clue to the faint uneasiness inspired by
this narrative that seemed to shape itself without human
lips in the heavy night-air of the river.

The night is fine, do you admire the view?

The moon was shining sulkily, because she thought the
sun had got no business there after day was done—

It's very rude of him, to come and spoil the fun!

We were cut off from the comprehension of our
surroundings; we glided past like phantoms, wondering
and secretly appalled...

Change in landscape.
Geology.
Tooth of extinct Horse.

White sand inscribes the waves.

Effects of a great drought.

Sandstone cliffs critique.

Parana.

Storm surges ignore.

Scissor-beak.

White sands frame the tsunami.

Kingfisher, Parrot, and Scissor-tail.

storm along the storied wave-washed place—

Revolution.
State of Government.

Excursion into the interior.
Profound ravines.

Waterfalls.
Wild useful plants.

    Missionary establishment.
    English weeds now run wild.

I'd like to retire there and do nothing
    (or nothing much)
forever, in two bare rooms:

    A loaf of bread, is what we chiefly need.

to read boring books, old, long, long books

    Pepper and vinegar besides, are very good indeed.

write down useless notes, talk to myself...

    Now if you're ready, Oysters dear,
    we can begin to feed.

Cut us another slice: I wish you were not quite so deaf—
I've had to ask you twice!

We could not understand because we were too far
and could not remember because we were travelling
in the night of first ages…

But— impossible.
The wind was much too cold to get that far
and of course the house was boarded up.

It seems a shame, to play them such a trick
after we've brought them out so far
and made them trot so quick!

The butter's spread too thick!

I weep for you, I deeply sympathize.

O Oysters, you've had a pleasant run!
Shall we be trotting home again?

On the way back our faces froze on the other side.
The drab, damp, scattered stones threw out long
shadows then pulled them in again.

Perforated pebbles.

Shepherd-dogs.

Horses broken-in, Gauchos riding.

Flocks of Butterflies.

Aeronaut Spiders.

Phosphorescence of the Sea.

Port Desire.

Bay of Islands.

Types of Organisation constant.

Change in the Zoology.

Causes of Extinction.

The lion sun walked the beach with the last low tide.

Compound animals.

Good Success Bay.

Return to the Ship.

Return to England.

Retrospect on our voyage.

// Epilogue.

Along the briny beach a garden grows. With silver bells and cockleshells, cockles and mussels, alive, alive oh. A coral orchard puts forth raucous pink blossoms. A bouquet of sea anemones tosses in the shallows. A crop of cliffs hedges a sand-sown lawn mown twice daily by long green-thumbed waves rowing in rolling rows. The shifting terrain where land and water meet is always neither land nor water and is always both. The sea garden's paths are fraught with comings and goings. Sea birds in ones and twos. Scissor-beak, Kingfisher, Parrot and Scissor-tail. Changes in the Zoology. Causes of Extinction. From the ship, the sea garden seems to glisten and drip with steam. Along a blue sea whose glitter is blurred by a creeping mist, the Walrus and the Carpenter are walking close at hand. A pleasant walk, a pleasant talk along the briny storied waiting in-between space. Wind blooms in the marram dunes. The tide far out, the ocean shrunken. On the bluff a shingled beach house sprouts, the colour of artichoke. On the horizon lines of tankers hang, like Chinese lanterns. Ocean currents collect crazy lawn ornaments. Shoes and shipwrecks, cabbages and kings. Water bottle caps and thick white snarls of string.

At dawn an ancient tractor crawls along the briny beach, harvesting the tide's leaves. The world's plastic. The sea's weeds.

SOURCE/CODE

J. G. Ballard, *Concrete Island*, 1974

Elizabeth Bishop, *The Complete Poems*, 1984

I. R. Butts, Laws of the Sea: *The Rights of Seamen, Coaster's and Fisherman's Guide, Master's and Mate's Manual*, 1857

Lewis Carroll, 'The Walrus and the Carpenter', 1871

J. M. Coetzee, *Foe*, 1986

Joseph Conrad, *Heart of Darkness* and *The Secret Sharer*, 1950

James Cook, *The voyage of the Resolution and Adventure*, 1772-1775

Charles Darwin, *Voyage of the Beagle*, 1838

John Davis, *Second Voyage Attempted for the Discovery of the Northwest Passage*, 1586

Gilles Deleuze, *Desert Islands*, 2004

Hernan Diaz, 'A Topical Paradise,' *Cabinet Magazine*, 2010

Eugene Field, 'Wynken, Blynken and Nod', 1889

Sir J. Franklin, *Narrative of a Journey to the Shores of the Polar Sea*, 1823

Martin Frobisher, *Third Voyage Pretended for the Discovery of Cathay*, 1578

Richard Hakluyt, *Voyages and Discoveries*, 1600

Edward Lear, 'The Owl and the Pussy-cat', 1871

Tom McCarthy, *C*, 2010

Nick Montfort, *Taroko Gorge*, 2009

Murray & Thomson, *Report on the Voyage of H.M.S. Challenger 1873-76*, 1885

Pet & Jackman, *Instructions and Notes Very Necessary and Needful to Be Observed in the Purposed Voyage for Discovery of Cathay Eastwards*, 1580

Lisa Robertson, 'disquiet,' *nilling*, 2010

R. F. Scott, *Journey to the South Pole*, 1923

William Shakespeare, *The Tempest*, 1610

Tacitus, *Agricola*, 97-98

Henry David Thoreau, *Cape Cod*, 1865

ACKNOWLEDGEMENTS

Portions of this work were created with the financial support of a PhD Studentship from Falmouth University, an Open Studio Residency from Struts Gallery, a Visiting Fellowship from the Eccles Centre for American Studies at the British Library, and an Exploratory Writing grant from the Canada Council for the Arts.

Portions of this work first appeared in print in *A Global Visuage*, *Arc Poetry Magazine*, *Code und Konzept: Literatur und das Digital*, *Fourteen Hills*, *The Goose*, *Journal of Writing in Creative Practice*, *The Other Room Anthology 8*, *Oxford Poetry*, and *para-text 4*. Thanks to the editors.

Web-based and live performance versions of the poems in this book have been presented, often in very different forms, in a wide range of contexts. For a full list of links, visit: Luckysoap.com/anoceanofstatic

Research for this book was undertaken at The British Library, the Marconi Archives at the Bodleian Library, the Telegraph Museum Archives in Porthcurno, and the Centre for Newfoundland

Studies at Memorial University in St John's. Many thanks to the librarians, archivists, and curators who patiently fielded my wide ranging queries.

Many thanks to the family, friends, collaborators, developers, editors, publishers, producers, performers, curators, and event organisers who have helped to chart this ocean of static in various ways, especially: Elisabeth Belliveau, Steve Boyland, Mez Breeze, Barbara Bridger, Tom Chivers, Aphra Kennedy Fletcher, Jerome Fletcher, SJ Fowler, Bertrand Gervais, Phil Hatfield, Tom Harper, Jhave, Peter Jaeger, Tom Jenks, Nathan Jones, Kurtis Lesick, Kay Lovelace, Nick Montfort, Erin Mouré, Camilla Nelson, Mary Paterson, Jörg Piringer, James Purdon, angela rawlings, Lisa Robertson, Ariane Savoie, Steven Ross Smith, Phil Stenton, Alice van der Klei, and Fred Wah.